BEHIND THE SCENES BIOGRAPHIES

WHAT YOU NEVER KNEW ABOUT

# SZA

by Kirstie Myvett

CAPSTONE PRESS

a capstone imprint

This is an unauthorized biography.

Published by Spark, an imprint of Capstone
1710 Roe Crest Drive, North Mankato, Minnesota 56003
capstonepub.com

Copyright © 2026 by Capstone. All rights reserved. No part of this publication may be reproduced in whole or in part, or stored in a retrieval system, or transmitted in any form or by any means, electronic, mechanical, photocopying, recording, or otherwise, without written permission of the publisher.

Library of Congress Cataloging-in-Publication Data
Names: Myvett, Kirstie, author.
Title: What you never knew about SZA / by Kirstie Myvett.
Description: North Mankato : Capstone Press, 2025. | Series: Behind the scenes biographies | Includes bibliographical references and index. | Audience: Ages 9-11 | Audience: Grades 4-6 | Summary: "What sport did star singer SZA compete in as a child? Which other singers has SZA written songs for? What are the names of her pets? High-interest details and bold photos of SZA's fascinating life will enthrall reluctant and struggling readers, while carefully leveled text will leave them feeling confident"— Provided by publisher.
Identifiers: LCCN 2024054900 (print) | LCCN 2024054901 (ebook) | ISBN 9798875210686 (hardcover) | ISBN 9798875210631 (paperback) | ISBN 9798875210648 (pdf) | ISBN 9798875210655 (epub) | ISBN 9798875210662 (kindle edition)
Subjects: LCSH: SZA, 1990- —Juvenile literature. | Singers—United States—Biography—Juvenile literature. | Rhythm and blues musicians—United States—Biography—Juvenile literature. | Composers—United States—Biography—Juvenile literature. | Lyricists—United States—Biography—Juvenile literature. | LCGFT: Biographies.
Classification: LCC ML3930.S995 M98 2025 (print) | LCC ML3930.S995 (ebook) | DDC 782.42164092 [B]—dc23/eng/20241119
LC record available at https://lccn.loc.gov/2024054900
LC ebook record available at https://lccn.loc.gov/2024054901

Editorial Credits
Editor: Carrie Sheely; Designer: Elijah Blue; Media Researcher: Jo Miller; Production Specialist: Tori Abraham

Image Credits
Alamy: Geisler-Fotopress GmbH, 19, Matt Crossick/Empics/Alamy Live News, 4; Associated Press Photo: Barry Brecheisen/Invision, 9, John Locher, 13, STRF/STAR MAX/Ipx, 29; Getty Images: Andrew Chin, 7, Frazer Harrison, cover, Gilbert Carrasquillo/FilmMagic, 24, Kyle Gustafson/For The Washington Post, 23, Larry Busacca, 27, Scott Dudelson, 15, Scott Legato, 11, Valerie Macon/AFP, 21; Shutterstock: Alena Divina, 20, Andrey Kozhekin, 10, Debby Wong, 16, ffoursesonss, 28 (house), imrajul hasnat, 6, JosepPerianes, 12 (pen), Juicy Fish, 13 (top right), Kbisuit, 25, KY726871, 20, 28–29 (hearts), Martial Red, 12 (scribble), mhatzapa, 26–27 (music notes), Yusak_P, 8

Design Elements: Shutterstock: Illerlok_xolms

Any additional websites and resources referenced in this book are not maintained, authorized, or sponsored by Capstone. All product and company names are trademarks™ or registered® trademarks of their respective holders.

Printed and bound in China.   006276

# TABLE OF CONTENTS

**Singing Sensation** ............................................ 4

**SZA's Skills** .................................................. 8

**SZA Soars** .................................................. 10

**A Splendid Songwriter** ................................... 16

**Growing Up, Family, and Friends** ...................... 18

**Overcoming Challenges** .................................. 22

**Helping the Environment** ................................ 24

**Inspirations** ................................................ 26

**Time For Fans** .............................................. 28

    **Glossary** ............................................... 30

    **Read More** ............................................ 31

    **Internet Sites** ....................................... 31

    **Index** ................................................... 32

    **About the Author** .................................. 32

Words in **bold** are in the glossary.

# SINGING SENSATION

SZA has worked with some of the biggest names in music. But it's her own music that has made her a star. In 2023, SZA was named Billboard Woman of the Year. With hit albums and a sold-out world tour, SZA is simply sensational.

SZA's real name is Solána Imani Rowe. She was born on November 8, 1989, in St. Louis, Missouri.

**What else is there to know about SZA? Let's find out!**

> **FACT**
> SZA is pronounced SIZZ-ah.

Are you a big SZA fan? Test what you know!

1. What is SZA's favorite movie?

2. What song did SZA sing Spanish lyrics for?

3. What alphabet did she use to come up with the name SZA?

4. What does she collect?

5. What are the names of SZA's French bulldogs?

6. What did SZA study in college?

**1.** *Pretty Woman*  **2.** "Fue Mejor" by Kali Uchis  **3.** The Supreme Alphabet  **4.** Crystals  **5.** Pepper and Piglet  **6.** Marine biology

# SZA'S SKILLS

SZA grew up in Maplewood, New Jersey. In high school, SZA was a talented gymnast. In her sophomore year, SZA ranked fifth in the nation. SZA's gymnastic days have ended, but don't challenge her! She once beat Olympic gymnast Simone Biles in a handstand competition.

# SZA SOARS

SZA started as an **independent** artist. She released her music on the internet. She signed with Top Dawg Entertainment in 2013. Her albums soon soared on the charts.

In 2017, SZA released her first album, *Ctrl*. It was on the Billboard 200 for 354 weeks! The next year, SZA had five Grammy nominations, but she did not win. Some of her fans were upset. Yet SZA focused on being grateful.

### FACT
*Ctrl* was named *Time Magazine*'s Top Album of 2017.

SZA released *SOS* in 2022. It reached number one on the Billboard 200 chart. *SOS* had more than 400 million **streams** in the U.S. during its first week. It went triple **platinum**. That year, SZA left the Grammys with an award.

SZA did her first arena tour in 2023. She toured worldwide, including in Australia, Europe, and South America.

> **FACT**
> SZA wrote more than 100 songs when working on *SOS*. Twenty-three songs made the album.

SZA won her 2022 Grammy with singer Doja Cat for Best Pop Duo/Group Performance.

SZA's numbers soar on social media. She has more than 20 million Instagram followers and more than 8 million X followers.

SZA's videos have impressive numbers too. The "All the Stars" video has more than 460 million views!

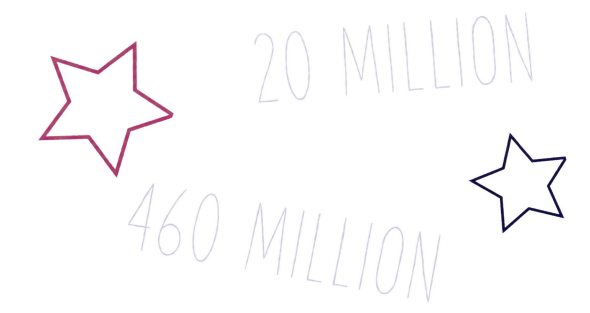

# A SPLENDID SONGWRITER

SZA's songs make her relatable to fans. She shares her feelings and **insecurities** in her songwriting. She has helped write songs for Beyoncé and Rihanna.

In 2024, SZA was **inducted** into the Songwriters Hall of Fame. She also received the Hal David Starlight Award. This award is for songwriters at the peak of their careers.

*". . . writing was where I felt like a person and that I had value . . ."*
–SZA, Songwriters Hall of Fame acceptance speech, 2024

# GROWING UP, FAMILY, AND FRIENDS

SZA's parents are Audrey Rowe and Abdul-Alim Mubarak-Rowe. SZA's brother, Daniel, is a rapper who performs under the stage name Manhattan. SZA has a half sister, Panya, too.

SZA's parents have different faiths. Her father is Muslim. Her mother is a Christian. SZA had a Muslim upbringing. She attended Columbia High School and a Muslim prep school.

SZA with her mother and grandmother

## FACT
SZA's niece Vans is also a singer.

Amber Wilson is one of SZA's oldest friends. They were roommates in college. Now Amber works as SZA's manager.

Singer Lizzo and SZA met many years ago on tour. They became fast friends. In 2020, SZA and Lizzo did a **meditation** session on Instagram for fans. They wanted to promote healing and self-care.

In 2024, Lizzo presented SZA with her Grammy for Best R&B song for "Snooze."

### FACT
Wilson and SZA wear matching necklaces that say *gratitude*.

# OVERCOMING CHALLENGES

SZA is loved by her fans worldwide. But she wasn't always popular. High school was tough. SZA experienced bullying.

In 2018, Columbia High School inducted SZA into its Hall of Fame. The students cheered when she went on stage. SZA shared her story of bullying. She encouraged students to daydream and follow their own path.

SZA performs at a concert in 2018.

# HELPING
## THE ENVIRONMENT

SZA cares about the environment. In 2021, SZA joined the groups American Forests and TAZO Tree Corps. They work for **climate justice**. One way is by replanting trees.

Racial **zoning** caused Black and some other communities to have fewer trees. SZA believes green spaces are important for everyone.

*"I need to be outside amongst trees, and among anything nature-based."*
–SZA, *Billboard*, 2021

# INSPIRATIONS

SZA gets ideas for her songs and videos from many places, such as classic movies. SZA is inspired by other artists too. She has worked with Kendrick Lamar, Doja Cat, Maroon 5, and others.

Kendrick Lamar and SZA

# TIME FOR FANS

SZA talks to her fans often. One fan, Sage Adams, sent SZA a message complimenting her outfit. Sage soon became SZA's creative director. SZA has even welcomed fans into her home.

# Glossary

**climate justice** (KLY-muht JUHS-tis)—the idea that people should be affected by climate change issues and solutions equally

**independent** (in-di-PEN-duhnt)—to do something free from control of other people

**induct** (in-DUKT)—to admit or bring in as a member

**insecurity** (in-si-KYUR-uh-tee)—a feeling of anxiety, fear, or self-doubt

**meditation** (me-duh-TAY-shuhn)—to do a focused mental exercise to help increase well-being and awareness

**platinum** (PLAT-in-uhm)—an album that sells 1 million copies

**stream** (STREEM)—to send or receive data such as music and videos over the internet

**zone** (ZOHN)—to create an area to use for a certain purpose

# Read More

Cooke, Tom. *Lizzo and Aretha Franklin: Queens of Soul*. Minneapolis: Lerner, 2025.

Kraft Rector, Rebecca. *Rihanna*. Mendota Heights, MN: North Star Editions, 2024.

Schuh, Mari. *What You Never Knew About Beyoncé*. North Mankato, MN: Capstone, 2023.

# Internet Sites

*The Atlanta Journal-Constitution: Get to Know SZA with These Random Facts*
ajc.com/life/get-to-know-sza-with-these-random-facts/OY3BBIJ4CTLBFQWUPD3OCXES3E

*Biography: SZA*
biography.com/musicians/a57628214/sza

*Kiddle: SZA Facts for Kids*
kids.kiddle.co/SZA

# Index

American Forests, 25

bullying, 22

Columbia High School, 18, 22

Doja Cat, 13, 26

environment, 25

family, 18, 19
fans, 10, 17, 20, 22, 28
friends, 20

Grammys, 10, 12, 13, 21
gymnastics, 8

Hal David Starlight Award, 17

Lamar, Kendrick, 26
Lizzo, 20, 21, 31

Maroon 5, 26
meditation, 20

social media, 14, 20
SOS, 12

Top Dawg Entertainment, 10
touring, 5, 12, 20

Wilson, Amber, 20, 21

# About the Author

Kirstie Myvett lives in the rich cultural and musical city of New Orleans. She enjoys foreign films, visits to the beach, and playing board games. Kirstie believes that representation matters in all places and spaces, especially in the pages of books.